The kind prince and other stories

Red Riding Hood page 3

The flowers in the wood page 16

The kind prince page 26

Rupert page 35

Nelson

Thomas Nelson and Sons Ltd
Nelson House   Mayfield Road
Walton-on-Thames   Surrey
KT12 5PL   UK

51 York Place
Edinburgh
EH1 3JD   UK

Thomas Nelson (Hong Kong) Ltd
Toppan Building 10/F
22A Westlands Road
Quarry Bay   Hong Kong

Thomas Nelson Australia
102 Dodds Street
South Melbourne
Victoria 3205   Australia

Nelson Canada
1120 Birchmount Road
Scarborough Ontario
M1K 5G4   Canada

© Macmillan Education Ltd 1987
This edition © Thomas Nelson & Sons Ltd 1992
Editorial Consultant: Donna Bailey
'Red Riding Hood' was written by Ron Deadman and illustrated by Sara Silcock
'The flowers in the wood' was written by Diana Perkins and illustrated by Gwen Tourret
'The kind prince' was written by Ron Deadman and illustrated by Ursula Sieger
'Rupert' was written by M. Morrin and illustrated by Julia Wakefield

First published by Macmillan Education Ltd 1987
ISBN 0-333-38399-0

This edition published by Thomas Nelson and Sons Ltd 1992

ISBN 0-17-422526-1
NPN 9 8 7 6 5 4 3

All rights reserved. No paragraph of this publication may be reproduced, copied or transmitted save with written permission or in accordance with the provisions of the Copyright, Design and Patents Act 1988, or under the terms of any licence permitting limited copying issued by the Copyright Licensing Agency, 90 Tottenham Court Road, London W1P 9HE.

Any person who does any unauthorised act in relation to this publication may be liable to criminal prosecution and civil claims for damages.

Printed in Hong Kong

Red Riding Hood

Once upon a time, there was
a very pretty little girl who had
a red cloak and a red hood over her head.
So she was called 'Little Red Riding Hood'.

One day her mother said, "Here are
some cakes for your grandmother.
Take them to her, but be very careful."

Now Red Riding Hood's grandmother lived in another village, so she had to walk through a dark wood to get there.
She was frightened, for in this dark deep wood lived a Wicked Wolf, whose teeth were as sharp as knives.
Suddenly, there he was, crouching above her. Red Riding Hood trembled.

"Woof! Woof! Grr..." said the Wicked Wolf. "And where are you going, may I ask?"

"I'm going to take these cakes to my grandmother," said Little Red Riding Hood. "Er... that's if you don't mind, Mr Wolf." She was very frightened.

"No," said the Wicked Wolf.
"I don't mind, my dear."
He knew that in the wood close by, there were men who were chopping down trees.
Those men had sharp axes.
The Wicked Wolf was afraid of them.
He wanted to jump on Red Riding Hood and gobble her up, but he knew he couldn't.
Not yet ...

He watched as the girl walked off through the woods.
Then he ran as fast as he could.
He was smiling, because he knew that he could reach the grandmother's house before Red Riding Hood could.

When he got to the house,
he knocked on the door.
"It's me, Little Red Riding Hood," he said.
"I have some nice tasty cakes for you, Grandma."
In went the Wicked Wolf.
The old lady saw that it was really Mr Wolf and she jumped right out of the window.

"Hah!" said the Wicked Wolf.
"How can an old lady jump like a cat?"
But Red Riding Hood would make
a much more tasty dinner, wouldn't she?

He smiled. "Yum, yum," he said.
He put on the grandmother's
nightgown and got into bed.

"Come in, my dear," he called when
Red Riding Hood knocked on the door.

Red Riding Hood was a little bit frightened.
Grandma's voice was so deep.
"Why is your voice so gruff, Grandma?"
she asked.
"I have a nasty cold," said the Wicked Wolf.
"Atishoo! Come in, my dear."
So Little Red Riding Hood went in.
There was Grandma, sitting up in bed.
Red Riding Hood was still a bit frightened.
She didn't know that Grandma would look so odd.

But she smiled and held out the cakes.
And then ... a big hairy arm reached out.

"Grandma, dear," said Red Riding Hood, "what big arms you have."

"All the better to hug you with," said the Wicked Wolf.

"And what big ears you have," said Little Red Riding Hood.

"All the better to hear you with," said the Wicked Wolf.

"And your eyes," said Red Riding Hood.
"What big eyes you have."
"All the better to see you with,"
said the Wicked Wolf.
He looked at the girl and licked his lips.
Yummy, yum, yum! What a feast!

Little Red Riding Hood was still frightened, but she didn't know why.

"What big teeth you have," she said.

"Yes!" said the Wicked Wolf.
"All the better to eat you with!"
And he jumped out of bed.

Little Red Riding Hood jumped too.
She jumped with fright and
ran as fast as she could out of the door and
into the deep dark wood.

"Hah!" snarled the Wicked Wolf.
He was very angry.
This was the second time that day
he had lost a tasty meal.

He ran after the girl as fast as he could.
Red Riding Hood could hear him
puffing and panting behind her.
Soon she was too tired to run any more,
and she fell to the ground, waiting
for the Wicked Wolf to pounce.

The Wicked Wolf stood above her.
"Got you," he said. "Got you at last!"
"No you haven't," said six deep voices.
The Wicked Wolf looked up and
he started to tremble.
There were six woodmen looking at him.
They were holding big sharp axes ...

The flowers in the wood

"When I was a little girl," said Susan's Granny,
"there were lots of flowers in this wood.
Just like it is today.
But one day something happened.
That's why there is this notice
'Please don't pick the flowers'.
Shall I tell you the story?"

"Yes please," said Susan.

I lived in a house in town with
your Grandad and your mother.
Many people came to visit this town.
Many people came to visit these woods because
there were thousands of wild flowers here.

In the early spring the woods were full of pale yellow primroses.
When the sun shone the primroses looked like pale gold.
The people from the town came to look at the primroses.

"I will pick a bunch for my Mum," said a young boy.

"I will take some home to my husband," said a young wife.

Lots of people came to look at the beautiful flowers and said, "I will pick a few to take home."

In the late spring the woods were full of bluebells. When the sun shone the wood looked like a blue carpet, because there were so many. The people from the town came to look at the bluebells.

"I will pick a small bunch for my Granny," said a little girl.

"I will pick some for the people in the hospital," said a nurse.

Lots of people came to look at the beautiful flowers and said, "I will pick a few to take home."

In the summer the woods were full of wild roses.
When the sun shone they opened
their pale pink petals.
The people from the town came
to look at the roses.

"I will pick a bunch for my friends,"
said a young man.

"I will pick a bunch for my teacher,"
said a small boy.

"I will pick a bunch for my bedroom,"
said a pretty girl.

Lots of people came to look at
the beautiful flowers and said,
"I will pick a few to take home."

In the autumn the woods were full of tall, white moon daisies.

"I will pick a bunch for the old man next door," said a young girl.

Lots of people came to look at the beautiful flowers and said, "I will pick a few to take home."

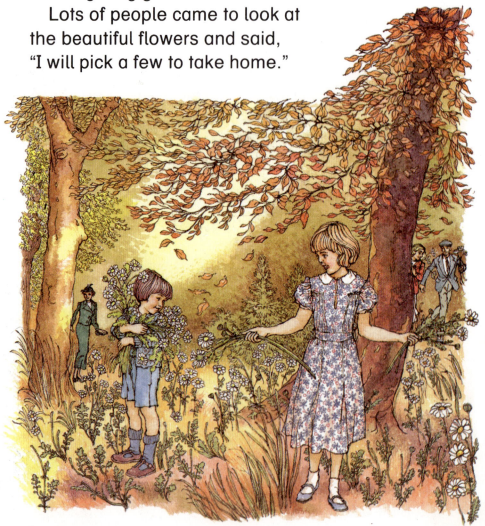

When the winter came,
the leaves fell from the trees.
It was too cold for any flowers to grow.
We stayed in the town.
We did not go out to the woods.
We waited for the spring to come.
Then we would see the flowers again.

At last spring came.
The trees had small green leaves
on their branches.
We all went out to the woods
to look at the primroses.
The sun shone through the trees,
but we could not find a single primrose.
"Where have they all gone?" we asked.
At last a little girl found a primrose under a bush.

Later that spring we went out
to look at the bluebells.
The sun shone through the trees,
but we could not find a single bluebell.
"Where have they all gone?" we asked.
At last an old man found one near a tree trunk.

In the summer we went to the woods
to look at the wild roses.
The sun shone through the trees,
but we could not find a single wild rose.
At last a young boy found one
climbing up a small tree.

In the autumn we went out to the woods
to look at the moon daisies.
The sun shone through the trees,
but we could not find a single daisy.
"Where have they all gone?" we asked.
At last an old lady found one near an oak tree.

We were very sad.
People had come a long way to see
the flowers in our woods.
Everyone had picked the flowers and
now there were only a few left.
"We must never pick the wild flowers again,"
we said.
"Perhaps one day our woods will be full
of flowers again, but not if people pick them."

So we put up a notice which said,
'Please don't pick the flowers'.
After three years, when the spring came,
the woods were full of pale yellow primroses
and bluebells.
And in the summer they were full of wild roses.

But in the autumn when the people saw
the moon daisies they said,
"We will never pick the wild flowers again."
And they didn't.

"So now we have all the lovely wild flowers in our woods, just like when I was a little girl," said Susan's Granny.
"Which flowers do you like best?" said Granny.
"The primroses," said Susan.
"And I like the white moon daisies best of all," said Susan's Granny.

The kind prince

Once upon a time, there were three princes.
They were brothers.
Two of them were cruel, rough men,
but the youngest was very kind and gentle.
Near their palace, there stood
an enchanted castle, where everything
had been turned to stone.
The horses, the soldiers, the king, the queen
and the princess were all stone statues.

One day, the three princes set out
to break the magic spell.
They came to a heap of earth.
It was an ant-hill and all the little ants
were running busily to and fro.

"We'll kick it over," said one cruel prince.

"We'll kick it to bits," said the other cruel prince.

But the kind and gentle brother wouldn't let them.

"Leave them alone," he said. "Don't hurt them."

Soon they came to a duck-pond and the cruel princes said,

"Let's catch the ducks and kill them."

"No," said the young prince. "Leave them alone. They are beautiful."

So on they went until they came to a bee-hive, where all the bees were humming and singing happily.

"Let's tip the hive over," said the cruel brothers. "We'll eat the honey."

"No, no," said the young prince. "The bees have worked hard to make their honey. Leave them alone."

Soon they came to the enchanted castle and saw the stone horses and soldiers all standing like statues.
But at a small table in one of the rooms there sat a tiny, grey man.

"I have turned everything to stone," he said. "You will never break my magic spell."

"Ah, but we can try," said the three brothers.

"Well ..." said the little man, "you must first bring me the thousand pearls the princess lost in the forest."

"Impossible," cried the two cruel brothers. "Pearls are small, and the forest is huge."

The youngest brother was smiling,
for an army of tiny ants had come hurrying and scurrying from the forest.
They were carrying the pearls.

"You helped us," they said.
"Now we have helped you."

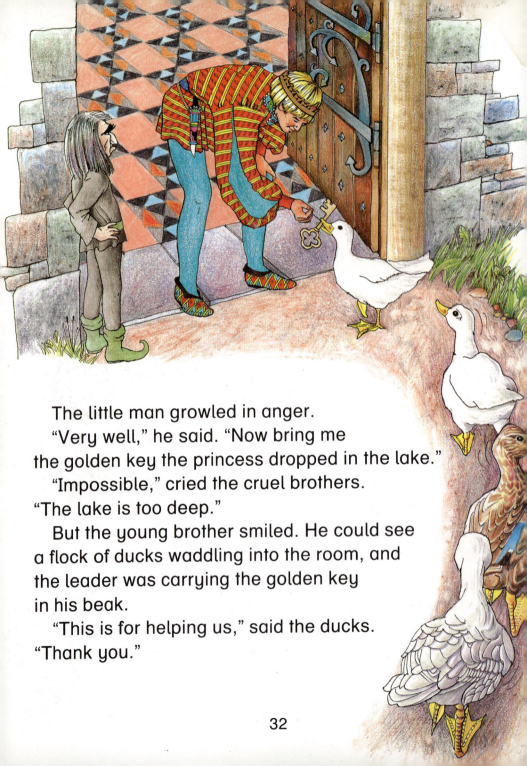

The little man growled in anger.

"Very well," he said. "Now bring me the golden key the princess dropped in the lake."

"Impossible," cried the cruel brothers. "The lake is too deep."

But the young brother smiled. He could see a flock of ducks waddling into the room, and the leader was carrying the golden key in his beak.

"This is for helping us," said the ducks. "Thank you."

The little man growled in anger. He laughed grimly and showed them three stone roses.

"Which one is real?" he asked.

The young prince smiled again, for a swarm of little bees had settled on the real, red rose.

"Thank you for helping us," they said. "Now we have helped you."

So what happened next?
The stone horses and soldiers came to life.
So did the king, the queen and the princess.
The young prince gave her the pearls, the key and the real, sweet-smelling rose.
The beautiful princess married one of the princes, and they lived happily ever after.
Which one did she marry? Do you know?

Rupert

Rupert was spoilt.
His parents thought that he was the most wonderful boy who had ever lived.
They always gave him everything he asked for.
He always got his own way.
He grew up to be a nasty, bad-tempered boy.

Rupert enjoyed playing games with other children as long as he won every time.
He could not bear to lose.
If he did lose he made a terrible fuss and he sulked.
One day, Rupert was playing a game of snakes and ladders with two of his friends called Tom and Bill.
He was determined to win.
The game was going well as far as he was concerned.
He was winning.

It was Rupert's turn next.
He shook the dice hard and threw it.
He had scored four.

If he got a four it would make him land on
the head of a long, winding snake.
He didn't like that at all so he decided to cheat.
Rupert counted 1, 2, 3, 4 but he only moved
his counter along three spaces.

This took his counter to the foot of a long ladder.
He screamed with delight and grinned as
he pushed his counter up the ladder to
the very top line of the snakes and ladders board.
Rupert only needed to move three more spaces
to win the game.

Bill and Tom looked at each other in surprise.
"Are you sure you did that right?" they asked.
"Didn't you score four, but only move your counter along three spaces?" said Tom.
"That's just what I thought," said Bill.
"No," said Rupert. "I moved my counter along four spaces. I started there," he said.
Rupert pointed to the space before the one where his counter had been.

Bill and Tom were sure Rupert had cheated but they knew that he would not admit it so they decided not to argue about it.

It was Bill's turn next.
He shook the dice hard and threw it.
He scored five.
Bill moved his counter along the board five spaces.
His counter landed at the head of a long winding snake.

He pushed his counter down the snake to the bottom line of the snakes and ladders board.

"Hard luck, Bill," said Tom.

"Serves you right," said Rupert.

It was Tom's turn next.
He shook the dice hard and threw it.
He scored six.

"Well done, Tom," said Bill. "You've got six."

"Oh blow!" said Rupert.

Tom moved his counter along the snakes and ladders board six spaces. It landed at the foot of a tall ladder.

He pushed his counter up the ladder to the very top line.
His counter was now only four spaces from the end of the game.

"You've got another turn Tom, and you only need four to win," said Bill.

"That's not fair," said Rupert.

Tom shook the dice hard and threw it. He had scored four.

"Well done, Tom," screamed Bill. "You've won."

"That's not fair," said Rupert. "You cheated," he cried. "I never lose – you must have cheated."

"No I didn't," said Tom. "You are just a bad loser."
"And what's more you are spoilt," said Bill.
"Then there must be something wrong with the game," said Rupert and he rushed off in a bad mood.

The next day, Tom and Bill were getting ready for an egg and spoon race when Rupert came along.

"Can I join in?" he asked.

"As long as you don't cheat," replied Tom and Bill.

"I never cheat," said Rupert.

The race started. Rupert found it difficult to keep up with Tom and Bill.
Soon he was trailing behind them both.
He didn't like this.
Suddenly, Bill dropped his egg.
"Never mind Bill," said Tom.
"Serves you right," said Rupert.
Then Tom dropped his egg.
"Hard luck Tom," said Bill.

"Good — I'm going to win now," shouted Rupert.
Rupert raced past Tom and Bill as
they picked up their eggs.
He was happy now as he was winning.

But soon Tom and Bill caught up with
Rupert and passed him.
Rupert was trailing behind them once again.
He didn't like it so he decided to cheat by
holding his egg on his spoon with his finger.
Now he was able to run much faster
without dropping his egg.
First Rupert passed Tom. Then he dashed past Bill.
He was happy again because he was winning.

Soon Rupert had won the race.
Bill and Tom looked at each other in surprise.
"I'm sure you were holding your egg on your spoon with your finger," said Tom.
"That's just what I thought," said Bill.
"No I wasn't," shouted Rupert angrily. "I didn't cheat, you are just bad losers."
With that Rupert rushed off smiling.

The next day, Tom and Bill decided to teach Rupert a lesson.

They began to play a game of football with some other boys when Rupert came along.

"Can I join in?" asked Rupert.

"No," said Bill.

"We don't like cheats," said Tom.

Rupert was very angry and he began to sulk. He asked the other groups of boys if he could join in their games, but they said no.

He sat down on the grass.
Why would no one let him play?
He knew it was because he cheated.
He wondered how he could win back his friends.
Rupert sat on the grass beside the football field.
He knew he would have to change his ways.
In future he wouldn't cheat and
he would let others win without creating a fuss.
Bill and Tom watched Rupert.
They felt sorry for him.

"Oh, all right, Rupert," they said.
"Come and join us."

"Thank you," said Rupert.

"Which side do you want to be on?" said Bill.

Rupert knew he must not win, so then they would know he had changed. So Rupert chose the weaker side. Tom and Bill looked at each other in surprise. Rupert had certainly learned his lesson. He was much nicer already.

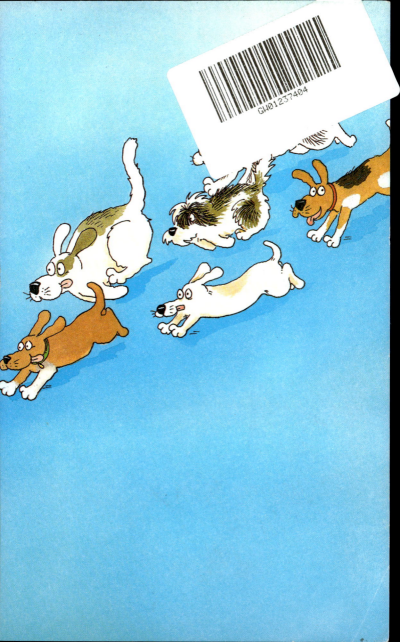

a note to parents

Little Owl Fun-time Readers are a delightful series of books of stories in rhyme which have been specially written to be enjoyed by younger children.

Read the rhymes out loud to your child at first, so that he or she can learn the rhythm of the words. Perhaps later you could encourage your child to read them for him or herself.

The Silly Sausage and other stories

poems by Lorna Bointon,
Clive Hopwood and Susan Lowndes-Butler
edited by Anne Hegerty

illustrated by Heather Clarke

Copyright © 1992 World International Publishing Limited.
All rights reserved.
Published in Great Britain by World International Publishing Limited,
an Egmont Company, Egmont House, PO Box 111, Great Ducie Street,
Manchester M60 3BL.
Printed in Germany.
ISBN 0 7498 0562 5

A catalogue record for this book is available from the British Library

The Silly Sausage

A big fat sausage, bought for tea
Came all the way from Germany.
He was a proper sausage too,
With lots of spicy bits to chew.

When Mother placed him in the pan,
That sausage he got up and ran.
He raced around the kitchen floor,
And screamed until his throat was sore.

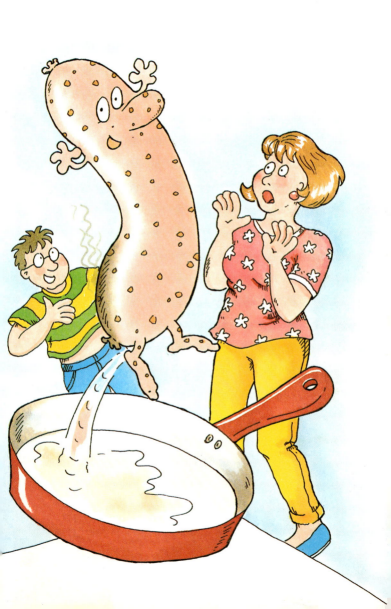

He wriggled, crackled and he spat,
He even scared the kitchen cat.
That sausage he would not calm down;
There seemed no way he would get
      brown.

He jumped and rolled, was never still,
That silly sausage roared until
My mother said, "There is no way.
We'll keep him for another day."

That sausage full of spicy meat,
He never will be cooked to eat,
He's in the fridge, so nice and chilly –
Our sausage wasn't all THAT silly!

Our Garden

The shed at the bottom of our garden
is a place I like to go.
It's full of stuff, more than enough
to make the garden grow.

We plant the seeds, we dig the weeds,
we shake the apple tree.
We harvest all the fruit and veg
and have them for our tea!

Helping Dad to Decorate

There's paint upon the ceiling,
There's paper on the wall.
Dad is decorating
My bedroom and the hall.

With rolls and rolls of paper,
And tins and tins of paint,
The smell is really awful –
It makes me want to faint.

A ladder holds the planks up
To paint the bits too high,
The brushes all need cleaning,
The paint is left to dry.

The paint is very messy,
As sticky as can be.
I help my dad to decorate –
But most of it's on me!

Shopping

I like shopping with my mum,
Buying goodies for my tum.
Fill the basket, lots to eat,
Savouries and something sweet.
Something special just for me,
And a treat to eat for tea,
Makes my tummy cry out YUM!
When I'm shopping with my mum.

Sidney Seed

Sidney was a little seed,
Who fell upon a patch of weed.
There upon the soft, warm earth
Was Sidney's shady place of birth.

The sunlight on that weedy patch,
Made little Sidney start to hatch.
Yes, he began to grow a root,
Followed by a tiny shoot.

Two tiny leaves began to sprout,
As Sidney's little head popped out.
Then through the weeds he grew so tall,
Till he was bigger than them all.

His leaves stretched out above their heads,
And they were in the shade instead.
His roots grew thick and strong, so soon
Those weeds found they had no
      more room.

As Sidney grew towards the sky,
The weeds, they all began to die.
They're dead and gone, that
      weedy crowd,
Now Sidney Tree stands tall and proud.

Get Well Soon

When I'm ill the doctor comes
And taps my chest, and pokes my gums.
She asks me if it hurts and where,
And prods me here and prods me there.

I've lots of cards to say GET WELL
And flowers with a lovely smell.
Everyone looks after me,
Better in a day – or three!

Kippered

"Oh dear!" said the Kipper,
"Here comes the old Skipper,
I bet he wants me for his dinner."
Sure enough he did bellow,
"I'll eat this fat fellow!"
The Kipper just wished he was thinner.

"If I had but one wish,"
Thought the poor little fish,
"It would be that I wasn't so scrummy."
But his wish came too late,
He was served on a plate,
A dish for the Skipper's vast tummy!

Why, Daddy?

Why won't the rain fall up not down?
Tell me why the world is round.
Where does the sun go every night?
And please can you leave on the light?

I need to know why dogs can't fly,
And lots of other questions why.
All these puzzles make me think.
And could I have another drink?

Why do plants and flowers grow?
And where do all the rainbows go?
And why won't money grow on trees?
And can I have a biscuit please?

So why do pigs have curly tails?
And are there fish that don't have scales?
Tell me stories, sing a song . . .
I'll fall asleep before too long.